Pebble Plus

Investigate the Seasons

Let's Look at Winter

Revised Edition

T0044786

by Sarah L. Schuette

CAPSTONE PRESS
a capstone imprint

Pebble Plus is published by Capstone Press,
1710 Roe Crest Drive, North Mankato, Minnesota 56003
www.capstonepub.com

Copyright © 2018 by Capstone Press, a Capstone imprint. All rights reserved. No part of this publication may be reproduced in whole or in part, or stored in a retrieval system, or transmitted in any form or by any means, electronic, mechanical, photocopying, recording, or otherwise, without written permission of the publisher

Library of Congress Cataloging-in-Publication Data
is available on the Library of Congress website.

ISBN 978-1-5435-0845-1 (library binding)
ISBN 978-1-5435-0873-4 (paperback)
ISBN 978-1-5435-0877-2 (ebook pdf)

Editorial Credits
Sarah Bennett, designer; Tracy Cummins, media researcher,
Laura Manthe, production specialist

Photo Credits
Shutterstock: Africa Studio, 5, Bakusova, 19, Dieter Hawlan, 1, FotoRequest, Cover, Jeff Thrower, 17, Jim Cumming, 13, Khomulo Anna, 3, Liubou Yasiukovich, Cover Design Element, Marina Zezelina, 9, Ondrej Prosicky, 15, Peter Wey, 21, SnvvSnvvSnvv, 7, tim elliott, 11

Note to Parents and Teachers

The Investigate the Seasons set supports national science standards related to weather and life science. This book describes and illustrates the season of winter. The images support early readers in understanding the text. The repetition of words and phrases helps early readers learn new words. This book also introduces early readers to subject-specific vocabulary words, which are defined in the Glossary section. Early readers may need assistance to read some words and to use the Table of Contents, Glossary, Read More, Internet Sites, Critical Thinking Questions, and Index sections of the book.

Printed in the United States 5594

Table of Contents

It's Winter! 4

Animals in Winter 10

Plants in Winter 16

What's Next? 20

Glossary 22

Read More 23

Internet Sites 23

Critical Thinking Questions 24

Index 24

It's Winter!

How do you know it's winter?

The temperature is cold.

The ground hardens.

Water freezes.

When snow falls,

it covers everything.

The sun rises later
in the morning.
Winter days are
the shortest of the year.

Animals in Winter

What do animals do
in winter?
Deer search for food
under the snow.

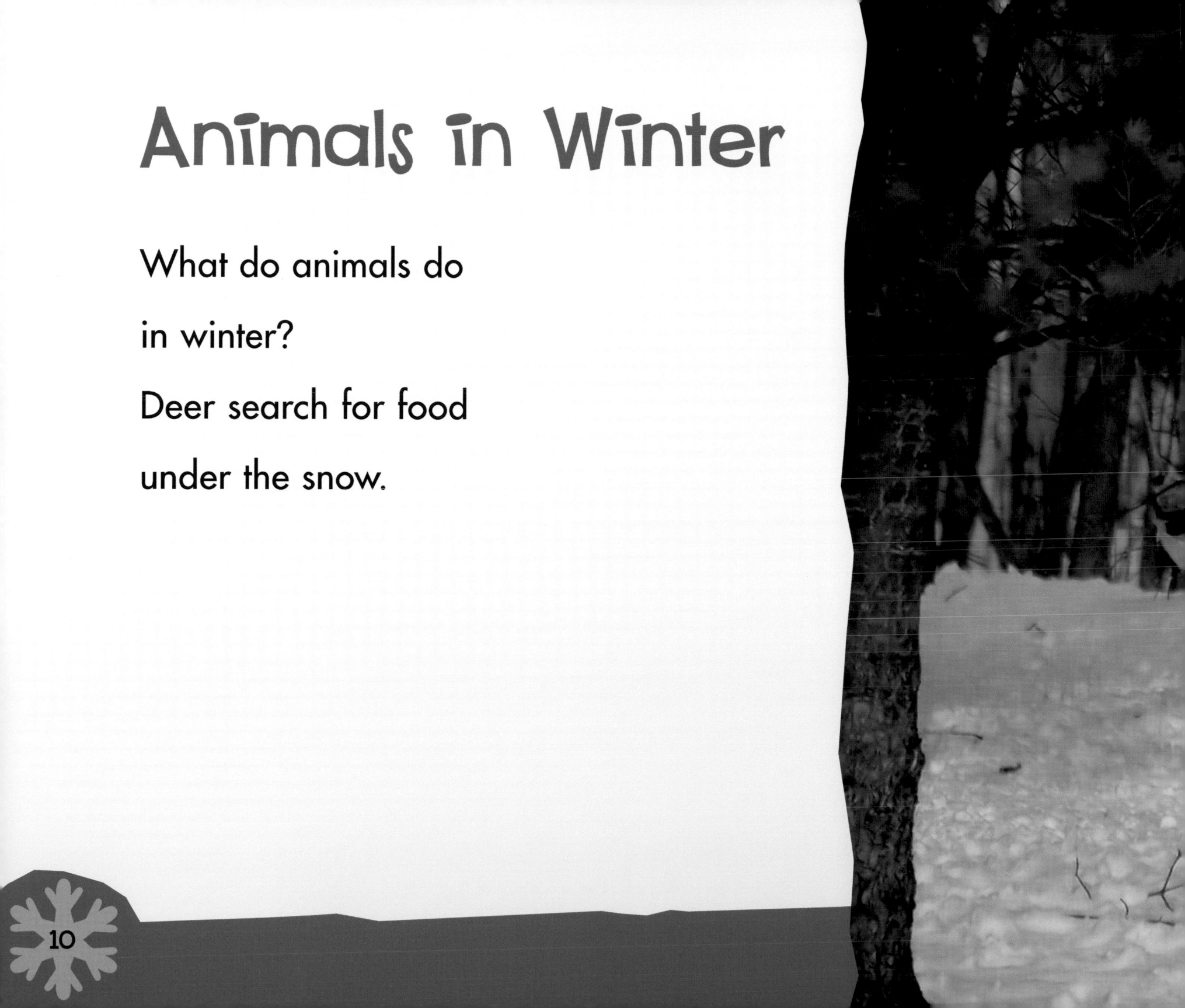

Some brown rabbits turn white.
Now their fur blends in
with the snow.

Owls sit in snowy trees.

They stay

for the whole winter.

Some birds migrate.

Plants in Winter

What happens
to plants in winter?
They do not grow.
Many plants look bare
and brown.

Evergreen trees stay green.
They keep their needles
all year round.

What's Next?

The temperature gets warmer.

Winter is over.

What season is next?

Glossary

bare—not covered

evergreen—a tree or bush that has green needles all year long

freeze—to become solid or icy at a very low temperature

migrate—to move from one place to another when seasons change

needle—a sharp, green leaf on an evergreen tree

season—one of the four parts of the year; winter, spring, summer, and fall are seasons

temperature—the measure of how hot or cold something is

Read More

Phillips, Dee. *Snowshoe Hare.* Arctic Animals. New York: Bearport Publishing, 2015.

Rustad, Martha E. H. *All About Animals in Winter.* Celebrate Winter. North Mankato, Minn.: Capstone Press, 2016.

Ward, Jennifer. *What Will Grow?* New York: Bloomsbury, 2017.

Internet Sites

Use FactHound to find Internet sites related to this book.

Visit *www.facthound.com*

Just type **9781543508451** and go.

Check out projects, games and lots more at
www.capstonekids.com

Critical Thinking Questions

1. How does white fur help some rabbits in winter?
2. What happens to the days in winter?
3. Describe what you like to do in winter.

Index

animals, 10, 12, 14
bare, 16
cold, 4
days, 8
deer, 10
evergreen trees, 18
food, 10
freezing, 6
fur, 12
growing, 16
migrating, 14
needles, 18
owls, 14
plants, 14, 16, 18
rabbits, 12
snow, 6, 10, 12
sun, 8
temperature, 4, 20